W9-CFB-404

Getting Creative With

FAB LAB™

Creating With

3D

PRINTERS

AMIE JANE LEAVITT

rosen publishing's
rosen
central®

Published in 2017 by The Rosen Publishing Group, Inc.
29 East 21st Street, New York, NY 10010

First Edition

Library of Congress Cataloging-in-Publication Data

Names: Leavitt, Amie Jane, author.
Title: Creating with 3D printers / Amie Jane Leavitt.
Other titles: 3D printers
Description: First edition. | New York : Rosen Publishing, 2017. | Series: Getting creative with Fab Lab | Audience: Grades 5 to 8. | Includes bibliographical references and index.
Identifiers: LCCN 2016017222 | ISBN 9781499465006 (library bound)
Subjects: LCSH: Three-dimensional printing—Juvenile literature. | Technological innovations—Juvenile literature.
Classification: LCC TS171.95 .L43 2017 | DDC 621.9/88—dc23
LC record available at https://lccn.loc.gov/2016017222

Manufactured in China

Contents

Introduction

A large red brick building on the Northampton Community College (NCC) campus in Bethlehem, Pennsylvania, is the home of one of the school's most state-of-the-art spaces. It's called the Fab Lab, or Fabrication Laboratory, and it's where students and members of the community can come and make all kinds of items, ranging from metal and woodworking projects to laser cutting, audio engineering, and 3D printing.

The Fab Lab's space is very industrial looking. Large tables are set up around the shop and each provides a place for creators to build and innovate. Machines of all varieties are placed throughout the lab—in fact, it's the machines that are one of the major draws of Fab Labs. After all, it's not just any kind of lab where you have access to expensive high-tech equipment like state-of the-art 3D printers, Sound Labs, vinyl and laser cutters, and 3D computer modeling technologies. At the Fab Lab, people may work alone on their projects but are encouraged to meet, chat, and collaborate with other people in the lab.

In a quieter space in the lab, professionals teach courses in a variety of disciplines—the NCC Fab Lab offers approximately eighty different types of courses. Jeffrey Boerner, the director of the lab, explains in a video on the lab's official YouTube page: "The Fab Lab is all about processes, manufacturing processes.

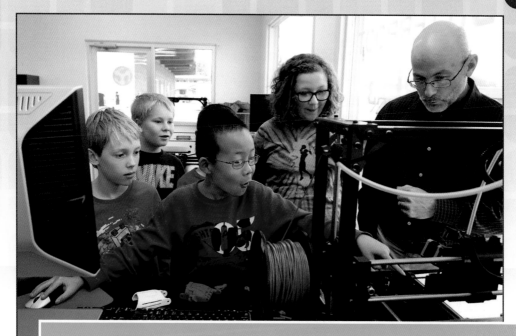

Seeing a 3D printer in action for the first time brings out the kid in everyone, including kids! Daly Elementary School students explore Bitterroot College's Fab Lab in Hamilton, Montana.

Everything from high-tech all the way to basic skills. You have to put those things together in order to build anything. We have the most incredible core group of craftsmen, especially instructors." One instructor at the lab has a master's degree in robotics; other professionals include experts in laser technology, wood turning, material design, and resin casting.

In the same video, Jessica Richline, one of the creators at the lab, explains why she frequents the lab: "The coolest thing about being here is the energy. It's exciting. They're building a robot here. There's three guitars being built behind me right now. It's awesome. Every semester brings a new group of inventors and creators and innovators, and it's wonderful."

The Fab Lab is an open community and everyone is welcome, no matter their age or ability level. One of the young people who creates at the lab is Derek Richline. In the YouTube video, he comments, "We are a Fab Lab. One of our slogans is 'Where Dreams Become Reality' and that is very important because anyone can just walk in here and make something. If you have a crazy idea, we can try it out."

The Fab Lab at NCC is truly a place where people can learn something, make something, and be inspired.

Chapter ONE

DIGITAL FABRICATION FOR EVERYONE

The Fab Lab at NCC might sound like a revolutionary, one-of-a-kind place, and to some degree it is. However, Fab Labs just like this one are found in many places around the world, and they're growing in number every year. But what exactly is a Fab Lab?

A Fab Lab is essentially a small-scale hands-on workshop that has specific high-tech equipment set up in an environment that promotes collaboration with others. The idea for a Fab Lab originated at the Massachusetts Institute of Technology (MIT). In 2001, Neil Gershenfeld—the director of MIT's Center for Bits and Atoms (CBA)—was teaching a course titled How to Make (Almost) Anything. In this class, students used the center's high-tech equipment to make all kinds of things, ranging from

All kinds of things can be made in a Fab Lab. Founder Neil Gershenfeld holds a piece of aluminum that has been precisely cut on a milling machine in the fabrication laboratory at MIT in Cambridge, Massachusetts.

a dress with sensors sewed into the fabric to an alarm clock that had to be wrestled to stop it from ringing. The students thoroughly enjoyed learning how to turn their ideas into actual products.

Expanding the Program

The class was such a success that the National Science Foundation decided to get involved. In 2003, they provided funding to help CBA start an educational outreach program. Smaller versions of the center, called Fab Labs, would be set

Fab Labs provide an ideal setting for STEM education. In this photo, a college mentor for the Learn 2 Teach, Teach 2 Learn program teaches students how to use a laser cutter at the South End Technology Center.

up in other locations. The first was slated for the South End, an inner-city neighborhood in Boston.

The two environments (MIT and the South End center) couldn't have been more different from each other. However, the students at both places were just as excited about the opportunity to create with the equipment. Gershenfeld recalled the experiences at the South End Fab Lab in an article he wrote for *Foreign Affairs* in 2012: "A group of girls from the [South End] area used the tools in the lab to put on a high-tech street-corner craft sale. . . Some of the home-schooled children in the neighborhood who have used the fab lab for hands-on training have since gone on to careers in technology."

FAB LABS, MAKERSPACES, HACKERSPACES, AND TECHSHOPS

As you learn more about Fab Labs, you will undoubtedly hear about Makerspaces, hackerspaces, and TechShops. It's important to understand that although there are similarities between these spaces, there are also definite distinctions between them.

- **Fab Lab** This is a trademarked name and is a franchise set up by MIT. These franchises are not for profit. MIT determines the exact equipment and training provided in each one. Fab Labs are also required to abide by specific rules at each location.
- **Makerspace** People are encouraged to engage in as many different kinds of crafts as possible in these spaces, including sewing, woodworking, and electronics.
- **Hackerspace** These spaces generally focus on electronics, computer programing, and repurposing hardware.
- **TechShop** These are also a trademarked name and not for profit. TechShops provide public access to a variety of crafting tools, including woodworking, welding, sewing, CNC fabrication, and machining.

Since that first lab in inner-city Boston, Fab Labs have been set up all over the United States and in many places around the world. In the United States, Fab Labs are found in dozens of states. They're built at colleges and universities, community centers, and even public schools. Fab Labs are also found in thirty countries around the world such as Ghana, India, Afghanistan, Ecuador, Israel, and Norway.

Fab Labs are located worldwide. This object was made on a 3D printer at a Fab Lab in Puebla, Mexico.

The small West African nation of Ghana was the sixth country to get a Fab Lab. It was set up on the campus of Takoradi Technical Institute. The excitement for the lab among the people of Ghana was equal to or greater than what was found at MIT and the South End. Amy Sun, an MIT graduate student, was one of the people who helped set up the lab. She was quoted in an MIT press release, in which she described the excitement among the students and how it kept growing week after week: "Students are taking [or have] just completed their exams and are coming to the lab begging to take a class or get trained on the equipment. Begging. No really, actually begging."

Gershenfeld weighed in on the same press release when he spoke about the purpose of the Fab Lab program. "Instead of bringing information technology to the masses, the Fab Labs bring information technology development to the masses," Gershenfeld said. "For our education and outreach efforts, rather than telling people about what we're doing, we thought we'd help them do it themselves. We've been pulled around the world by the voracious demand we've found each time we've deployed a Fab Lab."

Fab Lab Requirements

It's important to note that just because a place has a couple of pieces of high-tech equipment and a few people who like to create, the place can't be called a Fab Lab. In order to be classified as a Fab Lab, a location has to meet four specific requirements:

- Fab Labs must be accessible to the public. The whole point of Fab Labs is to give everyone a chance to design, create, build, and make. So a Fab Lab not only has to be open to

FAB LAB FEATURE: HAIFA, ISRAEL

Haifa, Israel, is home to one of the largest Fab Labs in the world. This lab was opened in December 2014 inside the MadaTech National Museum of Science, Technology, and Space. Fab Lab MadaTech was modeled after a Fab Lab at Chicago's Museum of Science. Both the Chicago and Haifa locations are the result of generous donations by the Wanger family of Chicago.

The Haifa location boasts 350 square meters (3,767 square feet) of space. It has one of the largest 3D-printing rooms in the world, with twenty-seven 3D printers, thirty-four digital design PC stations, two high-definition Polyjet printers, and six 3D scanners. Outside the 3D printing room, the Fab Lab also has vinyl cutters, a ShopBot, a CNC mill that can cut metal, and a dedicated room for woodworking projects. Lab manager Tom Sofer told a news reporter in 2015 that the purpose of the lab was to be a public institution dedicated to education, working "to ignite the next generation of hi-tech specialists."

Just like other Fab Labs, this location offers workshops and classes for all ages and ability levels. Children, teens, and

(continued on the next page)

(continued from the previous page)

adults can receive instruction on the basics of 3D printing and then go on to design their own objects at the design stations. As is true with all Fab Labs, the purpose of the Haifa location is to encourage ingenuity. As its website says, they are "looking for 'makers'—for whom 'do-it-yourself' is a motto."

An interesting feature in Fab Lab MadaTech is the furniture. Many pieces are the result of 3D printing. "Most of our desks were downloaded from the internet," Sofer told the reporter. Once the file was downloaded, the pieces were printed and then assembled. Little plaques on the bottom of the table give credit to the designer by name and web address. And on the top of the tables rests all of the lab's high-tech equipment. It seems more than appropriate to have a 3D printer housed on top of a table that was 3D printed, doesn't it?

the public, it must also be free to the public for a portion of its hours every week.

- All Fab Labs must have a specific set of tools, such as laser cutters, 3D printers, ShopBots, milling machines, vinyl cutters, computers with specific design software, and so forth. The reason that all Fab Labs must have the same machines is that it allows people all over the world to collaborate with each other. In this way, a person in Ghana who is working on a project on a 3D printer can network with a person at any other Fab Lab to get help or advice since they all have the same equipment to work with.

- Fab Labs must be part of a global knowledge-sharing community. In other words, all Fab Labs must be willing to communicate with each other and help with projects.

- Fab Labs must also agree to the Fab Lab's charter of rules found on their website. These rules include many of the things listed above. They also include such expectations as enforcement of safety requirements and openness to providing education for the community.

FROM SCREEN TO HAND

The 3D printer is definitely one of the most popular machines at Fab Labs. This revolutionary device—which makes many people feel as if they're living in a science fiction novel or movie—allows people to design something on a computer or scan something with a smartphone and then print a model or prototype of the object.

Three-dimensional, or 3D, printing is different from two-dimensional, or 2D, printing. With 2D printing, a picture of an object is printed onto a piece of paper. However, 3D printers produce a model of the real object. So, let's say you design a toy with special 3D design software. The screen shows you what your toy would look like from all angles—top, bottom, front, back, and sides. When you send this image to a 3D printer, the printer will create the three-dimensional toy using mathematical formulas calculated by the design software. In this way, you can quickly

Small 3D printers have become so affordable that designers can own them personally. In this photo, an artist is designing a pair of sunglasses using CAD software. Then, she'll print them out on her 3D printer.

go from seeing the image of something on the screen to actually holding the object in your hand. The amount of time it takes to print an object depends upon the complexity of the design and the speed of the printer. A simple key chain, for example, will take much less time to print than a model airplane.

3D-PRINTED GAMES FOR THE VISUALLY IMPAIRED

The Fab Lab at MadaTech in Haifa, Israel, offers educational outreach programs for area schools. During the 2014 to 2015 school year, students from a nearby high school took part in a weekly educational series at the Haifa Fab Lab. During this eight-month program, they worked on projects that, when finished, could be used by people with physical challenges. They created board games for the visually impaired that had words 3D-printed in Braille on all components. Also, other parts of the game that would normally just be a printed color (like triangles, plus signs, and circles) were designed to be raised from the plastic so they could be felt by visually impaired players. The students designed the pieces, memory game board, and cards using 123D Design software, which is an intermediate-level software. Then, they printed the pieces with a 3D printer using plastic as the medium. They also designed boxes and racks for the games using the SketchUp software and printed them in plastic on a 3D printer.

How Does a 3D Printer Work?

A 3D printer uses what's called an additive process. "Additive" means "something added to." This process is in contrast to the subtractive process, which means "something taken away." An example of a subtractive process would be carving or cutting. A milling machine is a subtractive device. In milling, you put a block of metal, wood, or other solid material on a milling machine and a rotating tool cuts and carves it into a specific shape. In 3D printing, nothing is carved or cut, but rather, the object is created by adding or stacking layers and layers of a material on top of each other. All of the equipment in a Fab Lab is placed into these two groups: they are either additive machines or subtractive machines.

Think about 3D printing this way. If a model of your body were being printed on a 3D printer, the printer would start out by printing the very bottom of the feet and then keep printing layer after layer until the entire body to the top of the head was printed. When it was all done, you'd have a small model that looks exactly like you! This recreation of a person's body is actually already possible using 3D technology. You can use a 3D scanner to take a 360-degree picture of a person. Then, you can send that file to a 3D printer and, voilà, the printer will make a small plastic action figure that looks exactly like that person.

The 3D-printing process works like this:

Step 1: A person designs an object on a computer using special 3D design software. Alternatively, a person scans all the way around an object with a 3D scanner to get a 360-degree view. In this case, scanners and smart device apps can also be utilized.

Step 2: When the design or scan is ready to print, the file is sent to the 3D printer.

Step 3: The printer follows the instructions in the design to begin depositing small amounts of a material into a very thin layer.

Step 4: Once the first layer is finished, the printer moves on to the next layer and the next until the entire object is printed from bottom to top.

Adding dimension to your prints

The words "printing" and "manufacturing" may become synonymous when 3-D printers become affordable enough for widespread home use. How a personal 3-D printer would work:

1 Products can be designed using 3-D software, bought in digital form or found free online, and then printed

2 A 3-D printer interprets the digital representation of the object and starts manufacturing it, one thin layer at a time

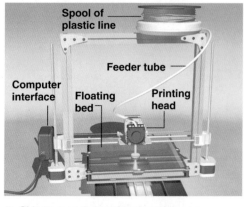

Spool of plastic line

Feeder tube

Computer interface

Floating bed

Printing head

3 As layer after layer of plastic is applied by the printer, the object begins to take form

4 Objects manufactured by the printer can take any shape and be any color

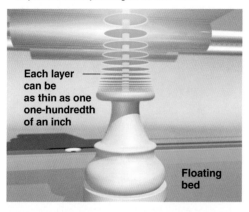

Each layer can be as thin as one one-hundredth of an inch

Floating bed

Designers can use 3D printing to take an idea from brain to screen to hand in a fraction of the time that traditional manufacturing takes.

As you're aware, a 2D printer uses ink to print on paper. But a 3D printer uses other types of materials instead of ink. The most common material used by 3D printers is plastic. Some advanced machines are able to use other types of materials, including metals, glass, wax, ceramics, rubber, nylon, sandstone, and, surprisingly enough, even food products and human cells.

The History of Printing in 3D

Three-dimensional printers are a rather new and affordable product on the consumer market, but they've actually been around since the 1980s. Back then, these printers were referred to as "additive manufacturing" rather than 3D printers. Additive manufacturing equipment was primarily used in industry and manufacturing. Designers could build prototypes and models and then "print" them with additive manufacturing before they created the official product. The main reason these machines were used this way was to save money. It was much cheaper to make a smaller version, or model, of a large piece of equipment before spending the money to build the real thing. However, the initial investment in these early machines was definitely not cheap. They would often cost as much as $250,000, with the plastic used to print the objects at around $800 per gallon. Obviously, in the early days, the average person could never afford to use such expensive technology.

The real breakthrough in 3D printing happened in 2007 when the device became more readily available to the masses. In that year, a 3D-printing machine was developed that sold for less than $10,000. That was still a lot, but much cheaper than it ever had been before. The primary goal at that time was to create a machine that cost less than $5,000, which has finally happened.

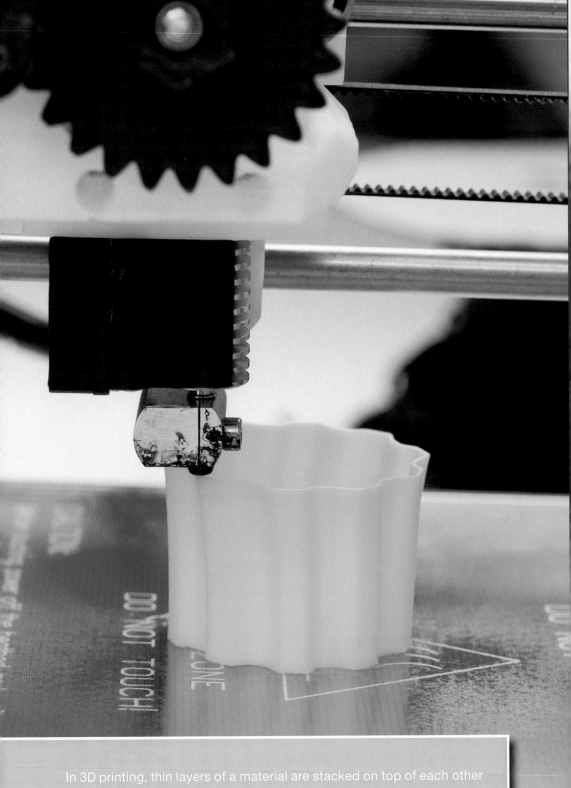

In 3D printing, thin layers of a material are stacked on top of each other until the 3D version of an object is formed.

As of 2016, inexpensive models can be purchased for as little as $400. Granted, these basic models have very limited capabilities; if you want to work on projects that are more advanced, you'll need to visit a community space such as a Fab Lab, which will have some of the higher-end machines.

One of the advantages of 3D printing, which is also called rapid prototype printing, is that it is print on demand. If you want to create a product using traditional manufacturing, you will usually have to order a huge number, perhaps ten thousand, of a product. That's because it costs a lot of money to make a mold of the object. Since 3D printing does not require a mold, you can choose to print one of an item rather than thousands. This allows designers to keep adjusting their prints to make better ones each time they print.

LIMITED ONLY BY YOUR IMAGINATION

Three-dimensional printing is truly limited only by your imagination. It's getting to the point that if you can dream it—and you have access to the right printer and printing materials— you can print it. There are many individuals, organizations, and companies already utilizing the benefits of 3D printing, and Fab Labs are a wonderful place to design and print projects.

Mind-Blowing Examples of 3D Printing

A simple search online will show you a variety of projects that people have made with 3D printers. The innovation of these projects will just continue to get better and better as time goes on. Here are some of the most awesome 3D projects that have been designed and created all over the world thus far:

3D PRINTING IN SPACE

When you're working on a project here on Earth and a tool breaks, you have to find a way to repair it or buy a new one. The same is true when a tool breaks on the International Space Station (ISS). Except, the main difference is that astronauts can't just run to the store and buy new tools. Instead, they must wait for supply missions to come from Earth, which could be months in the future. NASA astronaut T. J. Creamer explains on the NASA website that when he was on the ISS, a tip broke off a tool he was using. He had to wait from December 2009 until June 2010 for a new one to arrive.

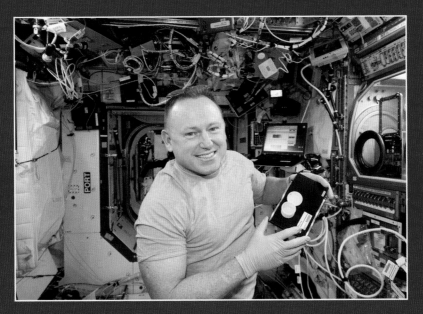

One of the first objects to be printed in space was a container with a lid, as shown here by NASA astronaut Butch Wilmore.

(continued on the next page)

(continued from the previous page)

Currently, NASA is trying to find ways that astronauts can be less reliant on Earth. One way to do that is to give astronauts the ability to build their own tools and supplies in space. That's where the 3D printer can come to the rescue.

In 2014, the first 3D printer was sent to the ISS. Before the printer was sent, twenty-one objects called ground controls were printed on Earth. On arrival of the printer to the ISS, the same objects were printed in the microgravity of space. The space objects were then returned to Earth for comparison with the ground controls. Engineers conducted a variety of tests to see if the objects printed in microgravity were exactly like the ones printed on Earth. Then, based on these initial trial prints, adjustments were made to the printer to improve how it printed in space. Currently, more advanced printers are being developed to enable even more advanced materials to be printed in space.

One of the great things about 3D-printing technology is that files can be sent electronically from Earth. Niki Werkheiser, NASA's 3D print project manager, explains on the NASA website that astronauts could "go from having a part designed on the ground to printed in orbit within an hour to two from start to finish." This drastically reduced the amount of time that astronauts must wait for materials and supplies. The plan is that when needed, they'll be able even to print a new printer in space so the entire system will be self-sustaining. Since this technology will help the astronauts develop self-sufficiency in space, it will allow them to travel even farther away from Earth—and maybe even someday to Mars. And don't just think that 3D printing in space is limited to tools, either. Plans are in the works to make 3D printing (and cooking) food in space a reality, too.

- The world's first 3D-printed car was designed and printed by a company in Arizona called Local Motors. This car was printed in 2014. They used a composite material of 80 percent ABS plastic and 20 percent carbon fiber. It took only forty-four hours for the car's body to be printed. Then, the car was assembled, with its tires and engine added on. By 2016, 75 percent of the car's body was 3D printed. The goal is to improve the design so that 90 percent of the car's body can be made on a 3D printer.
- In 2014, Hans Fouche in South Africa invented a lawnmower whose body and wheels could be printed on a 3D printer, with

In January 2015, this car was displayed at the world-famous North American International Auto Show (NAIAS) in Detroit, Michigan. It was produced entirely by a 3D printer.

the motor and blade added on. In February 2016, Andreas Haeuser from Germany designed another type of 3D-printed mower. While the same parts were printed as with Fouche's mower, Haeuser's ran on an Arduino Motor Shield. This turned the Haeuser mower into a robot. His device works like this: people place a wire around the area that they want to mow. Then, they set the mower down on one end. The mower starts to move, cutting the grass, and stops to redirect when it senses the metal wire. Traditional gas-powered lawnmowers can cost hundreds of dollars to buy. Then, a person still has to do the work of pushing or driving the machine. Haeuser's device is a more cost-effective option and requires less energy on the part of the owner. The instructions to print Haeuser's device can be downloaded from his website for less than $15. All you have to do after that is send the file to a 3D printer. Once the parts are printed, you can assemble your robotic mower.

- Believe it or not, clothing can actually be printed on a 3D printer. This is still a fairly new idea, but so far dresses, skirts, tops, jackets, swimsuits, and shoes have all been 3D printed. Danit Peleg studied fashion at Shenkar College of Design in Israel. As part of her graduate project, she designed clothing and then printed out her entire collection on 3D printers in her apartment. This was the very first clothing collection designed and printed at home. "I wanted to create a ready-to-wear collection printed entirely at home using printers that anyone can get," she explains on her YouTube video. She printed tops, skirts, jackets, and dresses. "I really like the result. It looks a little bit like lace and it moves beautifully," she says. All of the parts were printed in pieces, like fabric, and then she had to assemble them. Peleg feels that this technology

The 3D Print Fashion Show has been held in New York City every April since 2013. At this event, designers showcase their unique fashion ideas.

could revolutionize the way people dress, shop, and even travel. "Just imagine the potential. If you're cold, print your own jacket. Traveling with no luggage? Just print your clothes in the hotel room," she adds.

● All kinds of food have already been created on specialized 3D printers. Since this machine will be making things that people will eat, it has to be certified for use in commercial and home kitchens. The very first 3D printer for food was released in 2014. This printer could make chocolate and sugar treats. "The machine uses an ink jet print head that's

Even food can be 3D-printed! In an average of three minutes, this machine, developed by students at Tsinghua University in China, can print and cook a pancake!

just like the one you would find in your desktop 2D printer," explained Liz von Hasseln in an article in *Dezeen* magazine. "It spreads a very fine layer of sugar then paints water onto the surface of the sugar, and that water allows the sugar to recrystallize and harden to form these complex geometries." Since this first machine was released onto the market, more advanced models have followed that can print other types of food, including ice cream, pancakes, cookies, pasta, cake, and pizza. Some people believe that 3D printing is the way of the future for the food industry. "3D printers will potentially have the capacity to create an almost infinite amount of meals on-demand, quickly and for a fair price," Arthur Cassaignau wrote in "The Future of 3D Printing and Food."

In 2015, WinSun, a company in Shanghai, China, 3D-printed the very first buildings: a five-story apartment building and a 1,100 square meter (11,840 square foot) mansion. Huge pieces were printed on an enormous printer and then assembled into the structures. The printer that they used was 6.6 meters (21 ft) tall, 10 meters (32 ft) wide, and 40 meters (132 ft) long. The pieces were printed out of a combination of steel, glass fiber, concrete, recycled construction materials, and a hardening agent. The company estimated that it cost them $161,000 to construct the mansion. According to the *Washington Post*, the company has calculated that "3D printing technology can save between 30 and 60 percent of building materials and shortens production time by 50 to 70 percent," as of February 2015.

STEM AND FAB LABS

In the twenty-first century, science, technology, engineering, and mathematics (STEM) curriculums have been prioritized by administrators and teachers. Schools—from elementary grades through colleges—are encouraging their students to become more proficient in these subjects. There is a high demand in the workforce right now in these fields, and the demand is only expected to increase as time goes on.

Traditionally, these four subjects have been taught independently from each other in school, but that is not the case with STEM courses. A true STEM course incorporates all four of these subjects into a project. Most of the time, students don't even realize that they are using these subjects when they're creating their projects. They're too busy "making" to really think they're doing schoolwork!

For example, students who engage in 3D-printing technology use:

- Science skills, by choosing the right material for the project and making models;

- Technology skills, by using cameras, computers, software, the internet, and printers;

- Engineering skills, by figuring out problems with their designs and how to fix them or making designs that solve real-world problems;

- Math skills, by taking measurements, figuring out ratios, and converting data.

Students learn how to use high-tech equipment to create all kinds of revolutionary objects—including this hexacopter drone made at a Fab Lab in Kaliningrad, Russia.

The Importance of STEM

STEM courses are designed to help students think critically and solve real problems through creativity. In an article titled "STEM Education: Why all the Fuss?" technology entrepreneur Stephen F. DeAngelis states, "Educating students in STEM subjects (if taught correctly) prepares students for life, regardless of the profession they choose to follow. Those subjects teach students how to think critically and how to solve problems—skills that can be used throughout life to help them get through tough times and take advantage of opportunities whenever they appear." In addition, STEM education helps students look at the schoolwork that they are doing right now as something that is not only valuable to their own lives but also to the world. When you are building and creating a project that has a real-world application, it is immediately easy to see how what you are learning can help your life and can benefit the community as a whole.

Tim Jump, a STEM teacher at Benilde-St. Margaret's School in Minneapolis, explains how 3D printing has helped in the educational process at his school in the book *7 Amazing 3D STEM Projects to Do with Your Class:*

> I could talk to a student all day long about the importance of engineering design principles, but until they actually attempt to produce something on their own and encounter challenges and make mistakes, they won't really be learning. With the Dimension 3D printer, students are better able to experiment with their design concepts and test their engineering visions, truly understanding why a part worked or why it didn't. The printer has really changed the whole learning dynamic for my students.

K–12 FAB LABS

Some Fab Labs throughout the United States are actually located inside middle schools and high schools. Mahtomedi High School in Minnesota was the first K–12 Fab Lab in the nation. One student at that school, Brienne Francis, remarked about her experience in the Fab Lab in 2011 in the lab's YouTube video. She says, "The first week of school, I came home and I was so excited. I talked to my dad … about all of the machines and everything you can do with them and what I wanted to do. It was so surprising. I love it so much."

Tierney Putman, the teacher supervisor at the Fab Lab explains in the same video that most students "literally don't know how things are created. And to know that they can do it themselves using very simple software, they're amazed. The light goes on. A lot of them, I don't think they thought personally that they were cut out for engineering, but they're finding that they can do anything."

How Fab Labs Incorporate STEM

Fab Labs are a great resource when it comes to STEM education. After all, they are based on the idea of hands-on innovation through the use of design and technology. Fab Labs can be used by students as young as preschool age with adult supervision. Students don't have to have any real background knowledge when they walk into one of these labs. All ability levels are

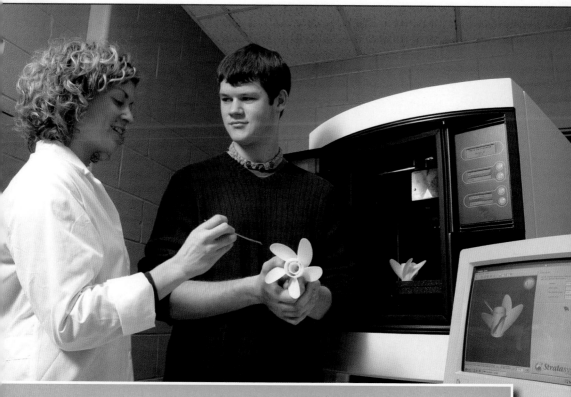

Students often collaborate on 3D-printing projects. Here, an instructor at Central Maine Community College works with her student to examine an object that they just 3D-printed.

welcome. Classes are taught on all of the machines and software. Even something as simple as the skill of measuring can be taught while projects are being created. If a student needs to figure out scale or measurements while they are working on a design, a helper or instructor can give them one-on-one help as needed.

The Champaign-Urbana Fab Lab on the University of Illinois campus held a summer camp for young "Thomas Edisons" (as they put it) in 2009. In this camp, the students created all kinds of projects in the camp, including things they designed on the computers and robots they made out of kits. The Fab Lab's website explains that the "youth came away from the experience

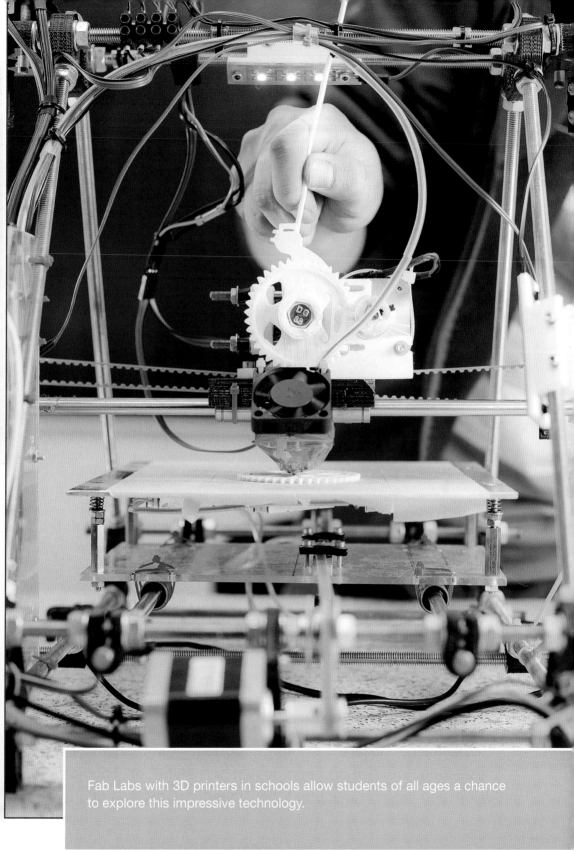

Fab Labs with 3D printers in schools allow students of all ages a chance to explore this impressive technology.

understanding a dizzying array of fabrication jargon, such as scope, proportion, rastering, and vector and—another plus— they had to use lots of math, in the summer no less."

Fab Labs help promote STEM fundamentals all over the globe. One of the main goals of Fab Labs is to help people create things that will solve problems in their own communities. Every community is different, so the things that each Fab Lab creates will likely be different. In South Africa, for example, Fab Lab creators made cell phone antennae so they could get better reception. In Norway, Fab Lab innovators made wireless radios to help them track their sheep. In Egypt, Fab Lab users have gained necessary technical and craftsmanship skills to help them become more marketable in the workforce. In Ghana, villagers come to the Fab Lab to make solar energy collectors and machines to mill cassava. STEM techniques are utilized every day by all Fab Lab creators regardless of where they live, how old they are, or what their educational levels and backgrounds are.

You Must Fail in Order to Succeed

One of the key elements of Fab Labs and of STEM education is the idea that failure is actually a very good thing. Jeremy Sambuca, former director of academic technology at Browning, says in an article on Makerbot.com that 3D printers help students by "making [them] more resilient. So that they can build confidence in themselves knowing that, hey, it's OK to fail."

Essentially, failure is an important component of engineering, innovation, and invention. Think of Thomas Edison and how many times he "failed" at his inventions before developing something that actually worked. This is no different when we turn to present-day machinery and scientific experimentation. When a product doesn't work, it gives the inventor a chance to analyze, reevaluate, and go back to the drawing board to make the product even better the next time. In fact, because 3D printers are capable of producing only one copy at a time, the process is actually quite forgiving for new experiments and inventions. The relatively low cost of 3D printing allows the inventor to keep trying until he or she gets it right.

3D PRINTER PROJECTS FOR ALL LEVELS

Creating a project in the Fab Lab on a 3D printer is an exciting task. For simple projects, an idea can be transformed into a real object in just a few steps. For more advanced projects, it takes a little more time and research and collaboration to go from idea to finished product. With 3D printing, you can create something you've thought of yourself, or you can find a project you like online, download the file, and then print the object. There are several different ways to go about printing your own projects, with a variety of approaches, which are outlined below.

To 3D-print from your own design, you need a few very basic tools. First, you need access to a computer with specific software (Photoshop, Illustrator, and 3D software like TinkerCad). Fab Labs often have their own software to use, so you will not have to sign up for an online version of 3D software if you use

STEM classes that partner with Fab Labs allow students to explore science, technology, engineering, and math in a hands-on environment.

the equipment there. Second, you need a digital camera or smartphone with a camera. Third, you need to have a sketch pad, pencil, and black marker. Fourth, you need access to a 3D printer either at a Fab Lab, at a community center or library, or even through an online company. Once you have these items, follow the steps described below. Keep in mind, these steps are just a general overview. If you need specific details on how to use certain programs or hardware, there are many more detailed step-by-step tutorials available online.

Steps for a basic 3D print:

1. Think of something you'd like to make. Go simple if this is your first product.
2. Sketch the object on your sketch pad. Start sketching with a pencil. Then, go over your final design with a black marker. Erase any pencil marks. Try to make this drawing as clean as possible. The black lines will be the outlines for your 3D print.
3. Take a picture of your sketch. Send this picture to your computer via email or the Cloud.
4. Open this file in Photoshop. Your purpose when using this program is to turn the picture of your drawing into a black and white image. Clean up all of the black lines so the outline is absolutely clean, with smooth, not jagged, lines. Save your file. Now, make a work path of your image. A work path will turn the pixels in the image into vectors. Vectors are mathematical data that will allow your image to be read as a 3D image later on. Save again. Now, export this file to Illustrator. Save.
5. Open the Illustrator file. Save the file as a .svg file.
6. Log on to TinkerCad, or whatever 3D software you are using. TinkerCad is a free app. However, you will still need to sign up for an account (if you meet their age requirements) or have an adult set one up. You may need to watch the tutorials on the site to understand the software. This is where you will upload your image from Illustrator, and you now get to see your object in 3D. With TinkerCad, you can adjust the length, width, and height of the object. Keep in mind that you'll be working in the metric system. Find a metric ruler to measure how big you want the object to be. If you were making a

pendant or key chain, for example, you wouldn't want it to be a meter in length! You can customize your object here by adding names or even movable parts. Be sure to save often; this is an online program and losing an internet connection could cause you to lose your work.

7. Once you are finished, you are ready to send your file to the 3D printer.

PROGRAMS TO USE FOR 3D DESIGN

TinkerCad is designed for novice users of 3D printers. A good program for intermediate users is 123D Design, with free software available online. Advanced users should consider the program AutoDesk Inventor, which can also be down-loaded on the internet. Engineers use this professional-level program to design products for the real-world marketplace, including cars, bikes, cell phones, computers, and even air-planes and robots! Not everything on AutoDesk has necessarily been 3D printed, but this same design software can be used for that very purpose. All of these programs have online tuto-rials that will show you how to use their software.

The Projects

Beginner:

1. Make a key chain.

You can make your own key chain using your own design, simply by following the steps outlined above. Or, you can find a file online for a key chain, download it, and then 3D-print it. Making a key chain is an easy way to get started in the world of 3D printing.

2. Make a pendant.

A pendant for a necklace is another easy project to get you started. Just as with the key chain, you can design your own pendant by following the steps above, or you may find a file online to download and print. A pendant makes for an easier starting project than many other types of jewelry, as a ring or bracelet needs to be sized to fit while a pendant doesn't need to be.

Intermediate:

1. Make a glider.

A glider is a plane without an engine or motor. Gliders can be made out of cardboard, paper, or—when 3D printed—out of plastic. Search the internet for "3D printing gliders" for some preliminary ideas. You can design your own on 3D software, but keep in mind that this will be a little more difficult than just finding a premade file.

For this project, you can't just expect to sketch out an airplane on a piece of paper, adjust it a little with software, and then print it. Before you can design a glider that will actually work, you must first spend some time learning about what makes a glider fly. You'll need to study wing design and figure out how to balance the body of the craft so that it has enough strength and is also light enough. All of this takes time, research, and investigation to find the answers.

2. Make shoes.

This might sound like it's straight out of a science fiction movie, but it's not: you can actually print out a pair of shoes using a 3D printer. If you decide to design your own, you will need 3D software. Be sure to take into account the size you need them to be in order for you to wear them. There are also project ideas available online.

Advanced:
1. Make a remote-controlled car.

Making your own remote-controlled car is a great use of your advanced 3D printing skills. There are many ideas online. These ideas will help you brainstorm designs for your own cars. *Make* magazine, in particular, has some great ideas.

2. Make a musical instrument.

There are a variety of projects online that allow you to make your own musical instrument. Guitars are a popular option. So are drums, flutes, and clarinets. Search "3d printing musical instruments" for some amazing ideas. You don't have to use these already-designed files, though. As an advanced 3D-printing expert, you could design your own.

FABRICATING A FUTURE

As time goes on and 3D-printing technology develops even further, we can expect to see more and more of our products fabricated closer to home, if not in our homes. Because of that, there is a growing need in the United States, in particular, for more students to be trained in this technology and in all the STEM-related skills taught at Fab Labs. Dale Johnson, a volunteer at the Mahtomedi High School's Fab Lab, explains the need for these types of jobs in a YouTube video, saying the Fab Lab "creates jobs in more than just engineers and scientists coming through and going on. It can also give skills to people learning how to run this process that are in demand right now in the industry. In fact, we met with three [people] in fabrication services and they can't get people who know how to run this type of equipment."

Neil Gershenfeld speaks with President Barack Obama during a meeting with students, entrepreneurs, and inventors at the first ever White House Maker Faire in 2014.

Fab Lab Employment Future

The US Department of Labor puts out information frequently to show what jobs are expected to be in demand in the future. Until 2022, there is expected to be an increase in the need for STEM-related jobs, including software developers, engineers, computer programmers, network architects, and so forth. Most of these jobs are expected to start out at a salary near six figures. So, not only will these jobs be in abundance in the future, they'll also be very well paid.

3D-PRINTING IN DEVELOPING COUNTRIES

Three-dimensional printing has many benefits in developing countries. For one, in many rural places around the globe, people do not have access to water near where they live. They thereby have to carry water by hand over long distances. Water cannot be 3D-printed, of course, and 3D printers cannot reduce the distance that needs to be traveled. But people can print buckets, bowls, and pails to help the people carry the water. Another use of 3D printing is to print the walls of green-houses. This is particularly helpful for people who live far away from markets so they can grow their own vegetables year round. The materials for solar panel beds can also be printed out on 3D printers, which can be used to provide people with clean sources of electricity.

A crucial way that 3D printers can be utilized in the developing world is by printing prosthetics, or artificial limbs. According to the NVBOTS website, it is estimated that thirty million people in developing countries require these specialized medical devices. One California-based company called Not Impossible has set up a 3D-printing lab in war-torn Sudan that specializes in printing prosthetics.

In late 2013, two RoboHands were printed in a Sudanese village for a fourteen-year-old boy named Daniel who had lost his arms when a bomb exploded in his village. Mick Ebeling traveled to the village from California. He not only 3D-printed the prosthetics, but also taught the villagers how to use the technology so more prosthetics could be made after he left.

On a video posted on the Not Impossible YouTube page, Ebeling says, "I still pinch myself that I was able to teach a group of people to print, many who had never worked with computers before and had never seen a 3D printer before, and I taught them how to make arms." The chances are very slim that Daniel would have ever been able to obtain prosthetics in any other way. The 3D printer has the opportunity to provide real change and improvement for people's lives in all corners of the globe.

Keep in mind that some STEM-related jobs definitely require a college education, but others do not. Some merely require that you know how to use the machines, design software, and have a creative and innovative mind. "There isn't a pool of people who know how to operate the software, let alone the hardware. Light manufacturing is coming to this class asking, 'Do you have students who can run this fabrication equipment?'" Tierney Putnam explains in a YouTube video about Mahtomedi High School's Fab Lab. The students using this lab are high school students, and they are being approached by business owners just because they know how to use the software and hardware available in a Fab Lab. Learning this technology and the principles taught in the lab can lead to job opportunities, and a very lucrative future in this industry is possible if a person is willing to go to college. As you'll notice in the chart, a computer user support analyst makes on average $46,000 a year, while a computer systems analyst with a four-year degree can make nearly twice as much annually, and a software developer makes two-and-a-half times that amount.

Kara Marr, age thirteen, was the first recipient of a prosthetic made by a 3D printer at the Independence Community College Fab Lab in Independence, Kansas.

A Better World Through 3D Printing

Not only can learning 3D printing and other Fab Lab skills help provide job opportunities and a good income, they can also provide opportunities to make a difference in the world. People in STEM careers are innovators and inventors. They create products that can change the world. Every product that you use in your daily life is the result of innovation. All of these items make life easier and more enjoyable for you and they also make life possible for others. Recent advancements in 3D printing in the medical field are astounding. Prosthetics, teeth, and even

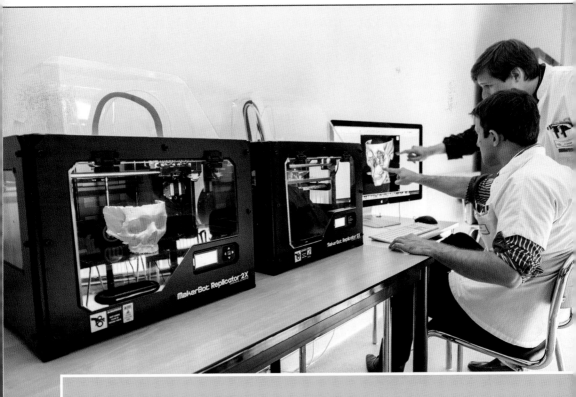

The medical community is utilizing 3D printing for all kinds of needs. In this photo, designers are 3D-printing the facial skeleton of a patient. With this model, custom implants can then be created.

human organs are being printed on these advanced machines. As time goes on, the items created on 3D-printing technology will only become more impressive.

Students in Kelly Hines's class in Greensboro, North Carolina, were swept up with how much 3D printing can impact lives as soon as they were introduced to the technology in their own classroom. "One of the first things that they saw on the MakerBot website was the man who printed a working prosthetic hand for his child … they said, 'Mrs. Hines, we should MAKE one of those,'" she explains in an article on CoolCatTeacher.com.

The question you must ask yourself is this: do you want to be part of this speeding bullet train of innovation and help usher in all of these amazing advances for humankind? If so, then find your local Fab Lab and get started. Your future in the world of 3D printing is sure to be not only bright, but also tangible!

additive A substance or material that is added in small quantities.

collaborate To work jointly on an activity to create something or solve a problem.

composite A product that is made up of many parts or elements of other products.

educational outreach program A program from the community that reaches out to schools to provide training or experiences, or a program from a school that reaches out to the community to provide training or experiences.

fabricate To invent or make something.

hardware The physical parts of a machine.

high-tech Something that involves high technology.

innovate To introduce a new idea, product, or way of doing things.

prosthetic An artificial body part.

repurpose To adapt a product or object for a different purpose than was originally intended.

robotics The branch of mechanical engineering that deals with the design and construction of robots.

self-sustainable The ability to maintain oneself with little help from outside influences.

sensors Devices that detect or measure a physical property and then respond to it.

software The programs that are needed for a computer to run and perform certain functions.

state-of-the-art Relating to the newest ideas and most up-to-date features.

subtractive Relating to a process that involves taking away material.

technology Machinery or equipment that was created based on scientific knowledge.

three-dimensional Something that possesses length, depth, and height.

tutorial Something that provides special instruction either in written or spoken words.

two-dimensional Something that has length and width, but no depth.

AssentWorks
125 Adelaide Street
Winnipeg, MB R3A 0A3
Canada
(204) 943-7909
Website: http://assentworks.ca

AssentWorks is a nonprofit fabrication lab that is dedicated to
providing hands-on opportunities for fabrication and
prototype development. It's a community of entrepreneurs,
inventors, tinkerers, artists, and innovators.

Change the Equation
1101 K Street, NW
Suite 610
Washington, DC 20005
(202) 626 5740
Website: http://changetheequation.org

Change the Equation is a nonprofit organization led by CEOs to
help encourage members of the business community to
work to improve STEM education in the United States. The
site includes ways that people can get involved as well as
success stories from schools around the nation.

Fab Foundation
50 Milk Street, 16th Floor
Boston, MA 02109
(857) 333-7777
Website: http://www.fabfoundation.org

This is the official website for Fab Labs. On this site, you can find all the information you need to start your own Fab Lab as well as how to find an already established one in your area. There is also a section called Fab Exchange, where "fabbers" can interact with each other and even find jobs.

Maker Media, Inc.
1005 Gravenstein Highway North
Sebastopol, CA 95472
(707) 829-1154
Website: http://makermedia.com

Maker Media publishes *Make* magazine, which is a great resource for all kinds of products for fabrication laboratories and beyond. The organization also has been instrumental in the conceptualization of the Maker Faire, first held in 2006, and is at the forefront of the Young Makers program.

Science Buddies
Sobrato Center for Nonprofits
560 Valley Way
Milpitas, CA 95035
Website: http://www.sciencebuddies.org

Science Buddies is a hands-on projects resource for students to use both at home and at school. There are hundreds of projects, an ask-an-expert resource, and information on science careers and current STEM happenings.

US STEM Foundation
7371 Atlas Walk Way #242
Gainesville, VA 20155
Website: http://www.usstem.org

This foundation was formed in 2011 by a group of parents,
teachers, and business leaders to provide students with
STEM-oriented extracurricular activities. A variety of
programs, hands-on activities, and other services are
funded by this organization.

Website

Because of the changing nature of Internet links, Rosen Publishing
has developed an online list of websites related to the subject of
this book. This site is updated regularly. Please use this link to
access this list:

http://www.rosenlinks.com/GCFL/3DP

For Further Reading

Anderson, Chris. *Makers: The New Industrial Revolution.* New York, NY: Crown Business, 2012.

Barnatt, Christopher. *The Next Big Thing: From 3D Printing to Mining the Moon. Amazon: CreateSpace Independent* Publishing Platform, 2015.

Bernier, Samuel N., and Bertier Luyt. *Design for 3D Printing: Scanning, Creating, Editing, Remixing, and Making in Three Dimensions.* Sebastopol, CA: Maker Media, Inc., 2015.

Drumm, Brook, and James Floyd Kelly. *3D Printing Projects: Toys, Bots, Tools, and Vehicles to Print Yourself.* Sebastopol, CA: Maker Media, Inc., 2015.

Gabrielson, Curt. *Tinkering: Kids Learn by Making Stuff.* Sebastopol, CA: Maker Media, Inc., 2013.

Harrington, Jesse, and Emily Gertz. *3D CAD with Autodesk 123D: Designing for 3D Printing, Laser Cutting, and Personal Fabrication.* Sebastopol, CA: Maker Media, Inc., 2016.

Hausman, Kalani Kirk, and Richard Horne. *3D Printing for Dummies.* Hoboken, NJ: John Wiley & Sons, Inc., 2014.

Honey, Margaret, and David E. Kanter. *Design, Make, and Play: Growing the Next Generation of STEM Innovators.* New York, NY: Routledge, 2013.

Kloski, Liza Wallach, and Nick Kloski. *Getting Started with 3D Printing: A Hands-on Guide to the Hardware, Software, and Services Behind the New Manufacturing Revolution.* Sebastopol, CA: Maker Media, Inc., 2016.

Lang, David. *Zero to Maker: Learn (Just Enough) to Make (Just About) Anything.* Sebastopol, CA: Maker Media, Inc., 2013.

Martinez, Sylvia Libow, and Gary Stager. *Invent to Learn:*
Making, Tinkering, and Engineering in the Classroom.
Torrance, CA: Constructing Modern Knowledge Press,
2013.

Wilkinson, Karen, and Mike Petrich. *The Art of Tinkering.*
San Francisco, CA: Weldon Owen, 2014.

Bibliography

Bureau of Labor Statistics. "STEM 101: Intro to tomorrow's jobs." *Occupational Outlook Quarterly*, Spring 2014. Retrieved March 29, 2016. http://www.bls.gov/careeroutlook/2014/spring/art01.pdf.

Caputo, Nicole. "7 Life Skills You Can Teach with a 3D Printer." Makerbot.com, September 15, 2015. http://www.makerbot.com/blog/2015/09/14/7-life-skills-you-can-teach-with-a-3d-printer.

Cassaignau, Arthur. "The Future of 3D Printing and Food." Sculpteo, November 11, 2015. http://www.sculpteo.com/blog/2015/11/11/the-future-of-3d-printing-and-food.

DeAngelis, Stephen F. "STEM Education: Why All the Fuss?" EnterraSolutions.com, May 8, 2014. http://www.enterrasolutions.com/2014/05/stem-education-fuss.html.

Eagan, Jessica. "3-D Printer Could Turn Space Station into 'Machine Shop.'" Nasa.gov, July 30, 2015. http://www.nasa.gov/mission_pages/station/research/news/3D_in_space.

Eskin, Blake. "MakerBot Stories: Wheels for a Middle School Drag Race." Makerbot.com, August 11, 2014. http://www.makerbot.com/blog/2014/08/11/stories-wheels-middle-school-co2-drag-race.

Fab Foundation. "Who/What qualifies as a Fab Lab?" Retrieved March 29, 2016. http://www.fabfoundation.org/fab-labs/fab-lab-criteria.Gershenfeld, Neil. "How to Make Almost Anything." *Foreign Affairs*, Nov/Dec 2012.

I-Stem Education Initiative. "C-U Fab Lab Fosters Creativity in Local Youth." Science, Technology, Engineering, and Mathematics Education University of Illinois at Urbana-Champaign. Retrieved March 29, 2016. http://www.istem.illinois.edu/news/fab_lab.html.

Journal, The. "7 Amazing 3D STEM Projects To Do with Your Class." Retrieved March 29, 2016. https://thejournal.com /~/media/1B15A181A74048FBB17D1303528C11A1.pdf.

Know, The. "China is 3D Printing Full Apartment Buildings & Mansions - The Know." YouTube video, January 27, 2015. https://www.youtube.com/watch?v=MbqfWN-9zHE.

Local Motors. "Watch Us Make History." Localmotors.com. Retrieved March 29, 2016. https://localmotors.com/3d-printed-car.

Mahtomedi HS. "FabLab – 'Make Almost Anything" – Mahtomedi, MN." YouTube video, November 15, 2011. https://www.youtube.com/watch?v=7rp1tc8rSgY.

Matisons, Michelle. "World's Largest 3D Printing Fab Lab Opens in Haifa, Israel at MadaTech National Museum." 3Dprint.com, January 13, 2015. http://3dprint.com/36673 /largest-fab-lab-opens-in-haifa.

MD. "Haifa Opens the Largest Educational 3d print Classroom in the World." Newsdrawer.com, January 11, 2015. http:// www.newsdrawer.com/haifa-opens-the-largest-educational-3d-print-classroom-in-the-world.

NASA's Marshall Center. "3-D Printing in Zero Gravity," YouTube video, August 12, 2013. https://www.youtube.com /watch?v=1Jwxn6EzW84.

Nguyen, Tuan C. "Yes, that 3D-printed mansion is safe to live in." *Washington Post*, February 5, 2015. https://www .washingtonpost.com/news/innovations/wp/2015/02/05 /yes-that-3d-printed-mansion-is-safe-to-live-in.

North Hampton Community College. "Fab Lab," YouTube video, October 5, 2015. https://www.youtube.com/watch?v= lj4v6-tpcb8.

Index

About the Author

Amie Jane Leavitt graduated from Brigham Young University and is an accomplished author, researcher, and photographer. She has written more than sixty books for kids, has contributed to online and print media, and has worked as a consultant, writer, and editor for numerous educational publishing and assessment companies. For a listing of Leavitt's current projects and published works, check out her website at www.amiejaneleavitt.com.

Photo Credits